Alfred's Kid's Piano Course
Notespeller 1&2

Music Reading Activities that Make Learning Even Easier!

Christine H. Barden • Gayle Kowalchyk • E. L. Lancaster

Alfred Music
P.O. Box 10003
Van Nuys, CA 91410-0003
alfred.com

ISBN-10: 0-7390-9245-6
ISBN-13: 978-0-7390-9245-3

Cover and interior illustrations by Jeff Shelly

Contents

Left Hand Finger Numbers 3

Right Hand Finger Numbers 3

Two- and Three-Black-Key Groups 4

The Quarter Note 5

The Quarter Rest 6

The Half Note 7

The Whole Note 8

White Keys 9

Finding C, D, and E on the Keyboard 10

Finding A and B on the Keyboard 11

White Key Review: C, D, E 11

The Whole Rest 12

Finding F and G on the Keyboard 13

White Key Review: F, G, A, B 13

The 4/4 Time Signature 14

The Dotted Half Note .15

The 3/4 Time Signature 15

Review 16

The Staff 17

The Treble Clef 18

The Bass Clef 19

Skips 20

The Grand Staff 21

The Half Rest 22

Middle C Position for LH 23

Middle C Position for RH 24

C Position for LH 25

C Position on the Grand Staff 26

More C Position on the Grand Staff 27

Middle C Position on the Grand Staff 28

More Middle C Position on the Grand Staff 29

C Position Review 30

Review 31

2nds 32

3rds 33

Melodic Intervals 34

Harmonic Intervals 35

4ths 36

Note and Interval Review 37

5ths 38

Note and Interval Review 39

G-A-B in Treble Clef 40

G-A-B in Bass Clef 41

G Position for RH 42

G Position for LH 43

G Position on the Grand Staff 44

Flat 45

Sharp 46

Note and Interval Review in Treble Clef 47

Note and Interval Review in Bass Clef 48

Left Hand Finger Numbers

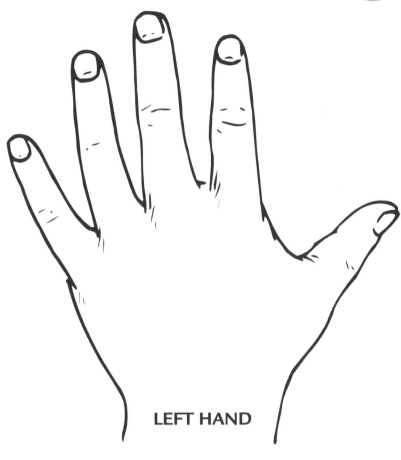

LEFT HAND

1. Color finger 1 **red.**
2. Color finger 2 **blue.**
3. Color finger 3 **purple.**
4. Color finger 4 **green.**
5. Color finger 5 **brown.**

Right Hand Finger Numbers

1. Color finger 1 **red.**
2. Color finger 2 **blue.**
3. Color finger 3 **purple.**
4. Color finger 4 **green.**
5. Color finger 5 **brown.**

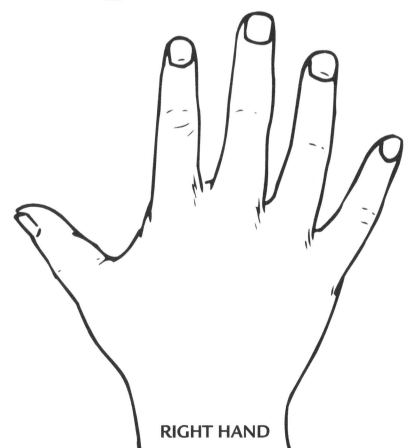

RIGHT HAND

Use with Book 1, page 7.

Two- and Three-Black-Key Groups

- Circle each two-black-key group with a **blue** crayon.
- Circle each three-black-key group with a **red** crayon.

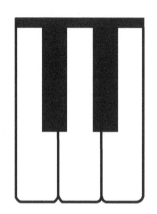

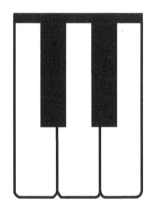

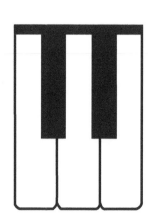
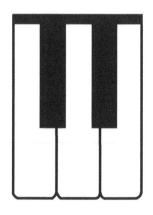

The Quarter Note

A *quarter note* has a black notehead and a stem.
Each quarter note gets one count.

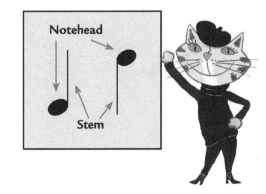

How to Draw Quarter Notes

Step 1:   Create noteheads by tracing the ovals and coloring them black.

Step 2:   Create the stems. For the first three notes, trace the lines going down from the left of the noteheads. For the second three notes, trace the stems going up from the right of the noteheads.

Draw four more quarter notes with stems going down.

Draw four more quarter notes with stems going up.

Loud and Soft Sounds

1. The sign *p (piano)* means to play   loud.
    soft.
    circle one

2. The sign *f (forte)* means to play   loud.
    soft.
    circle one

Use with Book 1, page 11.

The Quarter Rest

The *quarter rest* means to be silent for one count.

How to Draw Quarter Rests

Step 1: Trace the short lines slanting down from left to right.

Step 2: Trace the longer lines slanting down from right to left.

Step 3: Trace the other short lines slanting down from left to right.

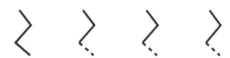

Step 4: Trace the curled lines, almost like a letter "c."

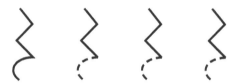

Draw four more quarter rests.

Black-Key Groups

1. This is a two-/three- black-key group.
   circle one

2. This is a two-/three- black-key group.
   circle one

The Half Note

A *half note* gets two counts. It is twice as long as a quarter note.

How to Draw Half Notes

Step 1: Create noteheads by tracing the ovals

Step 2: Create the stems. For the first three notes, trace the stems going down from the left of the noteheads. For the second three notes, trace the stems going up from the right of the noteheads.

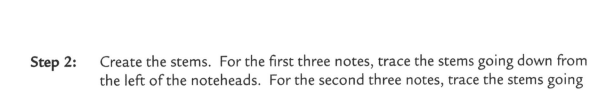

Draw four more half notes with stems going down.

Draw four more half notes with stems going up.

Use with Book 1, page 13.

The Whole Note

A *whole note* gets four counts.

How to Draw Whole Notes

Create whole notes by tracing the ovals.

Note Review

1. Circle the name of each note. Then write the number of counts it gets on the blank line.

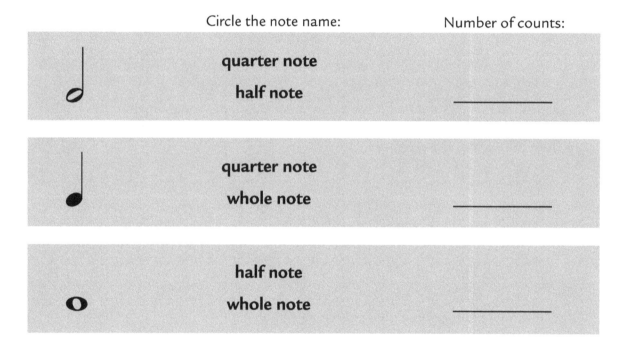

	Circle the note name:	Number of counts:
	quarter note **half note**	_____
	quarter note whole note	_____
	half note whole note	_____

2. Circle each whole note with a **green** crayon.
   Circle each half note with a **blue** crayon.
   Circle each quarter note with a **red** crayon.

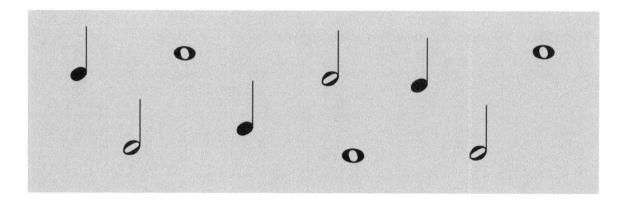

White Keys

Piano keys are named for the first seven letters of the alphabet.

A B C D E F G

1. Write the missing letter names from the music alphabet on each line.

   • <u>A</u>   <u> </u>   <u>C</u>   <u> </u>   <u>E</u>   <u> </u>   <u>G</u>

   • <u> </u>   <u>B</u>   <u> </u>   <u> </u>   <u>E</u>   <u>F</u>   <u> </u>

2. Write the name of every white key on the keyboard, beginning with the given A.

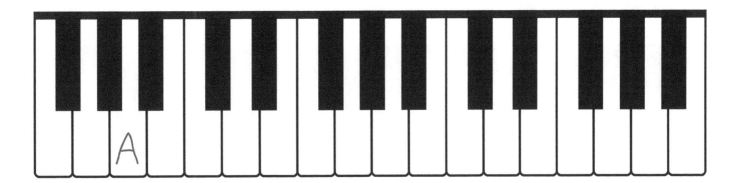

3. Write the letter name on each key marked X.

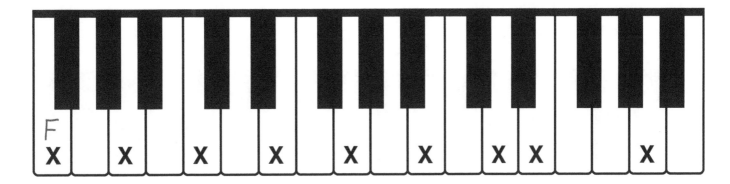

Use with Book 1, page 17.

Finding C, D, and E on the Keyboard

1. Color the HIGHEST C **green.**
2. Color the LOWEST C **purple.**
3. Color the other C's **brown.**

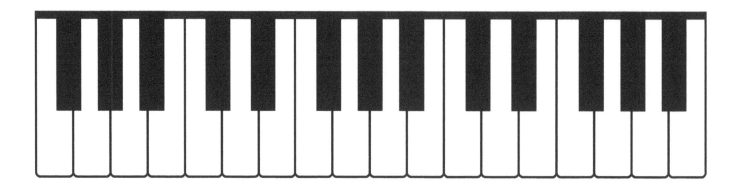

4. Color the HIGHEST D **red.**
5. Color the LOWEST D **yellow.**
6. Color the other D's **blue.**

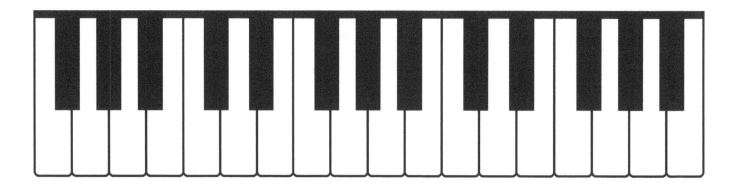

7. Color the HIGHEST E **pink.**
8. Color the LOWEST E **orange.**
9. Color the other E's **green.**

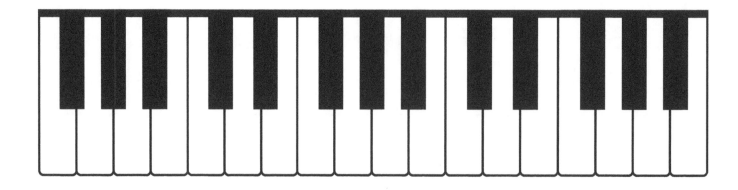

Finding A and B on the Keyboard

1. Color the HIGHEST A **green.**
2. Color the LOWEST A **purple.**
3. Color the other A's **brown.**

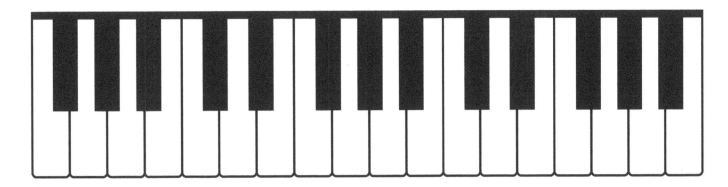

4. Color the HIGHEST B **red.**
5. Color the LOWEST B **yellow.**
6. Color the other B's **blue.**

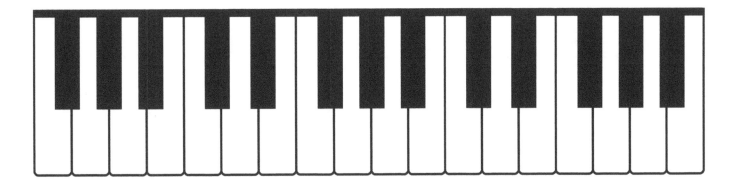

White Key Review: C, D, E

1. Color each C **yellow.**
2. Color each D **brown.**
3. Color each E **purple.**

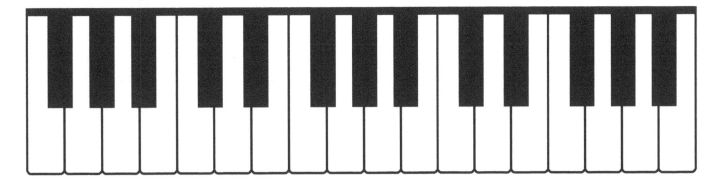

The Whole Rest

A *whole rest* gets four counts.

Do not play for the entire measure.

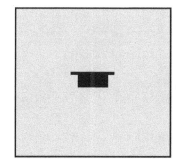

How to Draw Whole Rests

Step 1: Trace the boxes hanging from short line.

Step 2: Fill in the boxes.

Step 3: Draw four more whole rests.

Note Review

Draw the following notes:

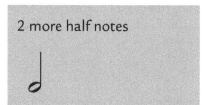

2 more quarter notes

2 more half notes

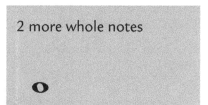

2 more whole notes

Finding F and G on the Keyboard

1. Color the HIGHEST F **pink.**
2. Color the LOWEST F **orange.**
3. Color the other F's **green.**

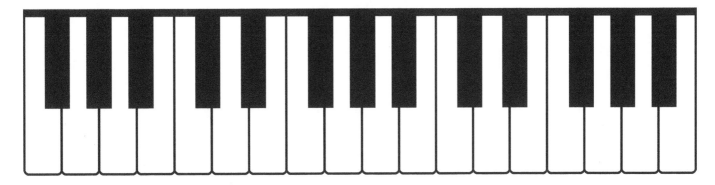

4. Color the HIGHEST G **red.**
5. Color the LOWEST G **yellow.**
6. Color the other G's **blue.**

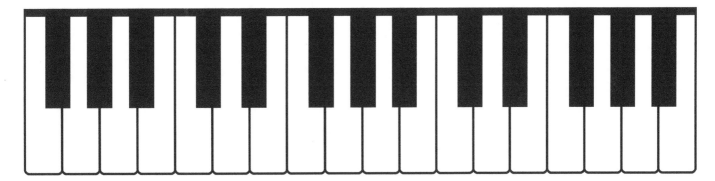

White Key Review: F, G, A, B

1. Color each F **green.**
2. Color each G **red.**
3. Color each A **blue.**
4. Color each B **purple.**

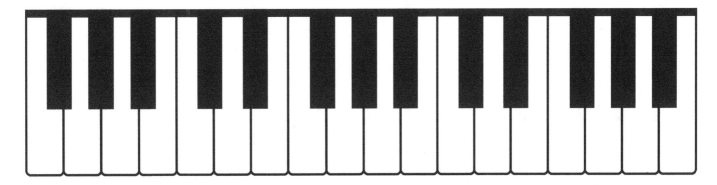

Use with Book 1, page 26.

The 4/4 Time Signature

A 4/4 time signature means there are four equal beats in every measure.

How to Draw the 4/4 Time Signature

Step 1: Trace the number "4."   4   4   4   4

Step 2: Trace the second "4" below the first one.

4/4   4/4   4/4   4/4

Draw four more 4/4 time signatures.

4/4

Note Review

Complete each measure by drawing the correct note (♩, ♩, or o) in the measure. Each measure should have four beats.

1.

2.

3.

4.

The Dotted Half Note

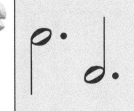

The *dotted half note* gets three counts.

How to Draw the Dotted Half Note

Step 1: Trace the half notes.

Step 2: Trace the dot to the right of each notehead.

Draw three more dotted half notes with stems going up and three dotted half notes with stems going down.

The 3/4 Time Signature

A 3/4 time signature means there are three equal beats in every measure.

How to Draw the 3/4 Time Signature

Step 1: Trace the number "3."

3 3 3 3

Step 2: Trace the number "4" below the number 3.

Draw four more 3/4 time signatures.

Use with Book 1, page 28.

Review

Draw a line connecting the dots to match the symbol to its name.

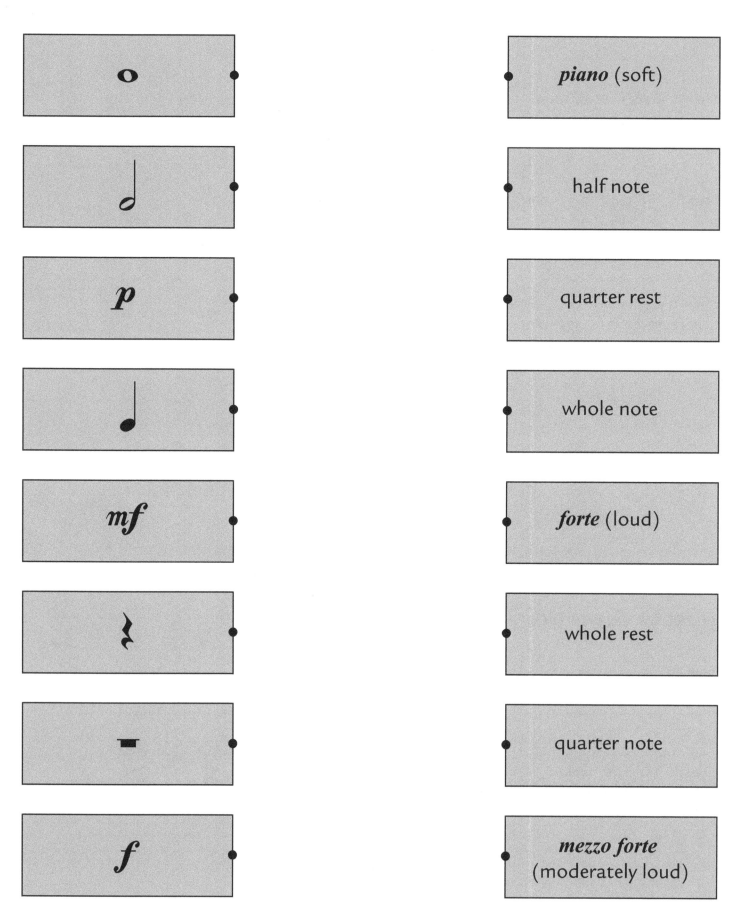

o	*piano* (soft)
𝅗𝅥	half note
p	quarter rest
𝅘𝅥	whole note
mf	*forte* (loud)
𝄽	whole rest
𝄻	quarter note
f	*mezzo forte* (moderately loud)

The Staff

Music is written on a STAFF of 5 lines and 4 spaces.

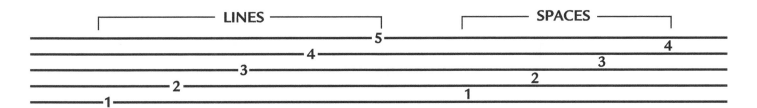

Some notes are written on LINES.

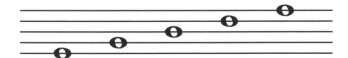

Some notes are written in SPACES.

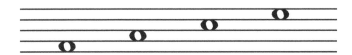

1. Circle each LINE NOTE.

2. Circle each SPACE NOTE.

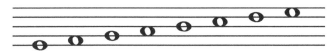

3. Name the line for each note in the box below the staff.

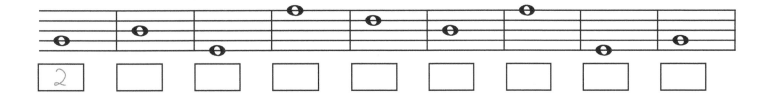

4. Name the space for each note in the box below the staff.

The Treble Clef

Use with Book 1, page 31.

The TREBLE CLEF SIGN 𝄞 locates the G above the middle of the keyboard.

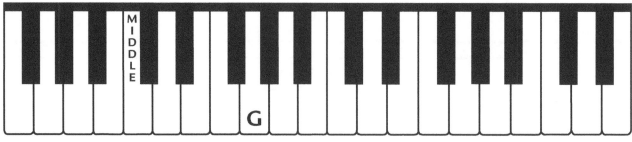

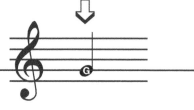

This is the G line.   The clef sign curls around the G line.

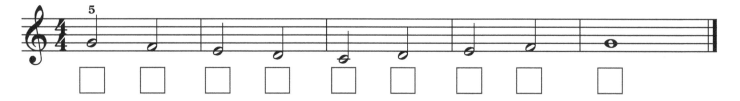

By moving up or down from the G line,
you can name any note on the treble staff.

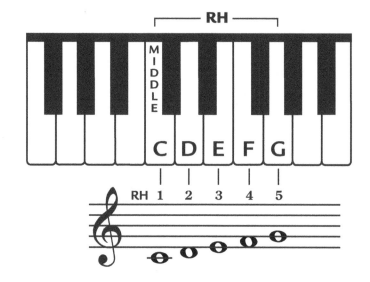

1. Write the name of each note in the square below it. Then play and say the note names.

□ □ □ □ □ □ □ □

2. Write the name of each note in the square below it. The letters in each group
   of squares will spell a familiar word.

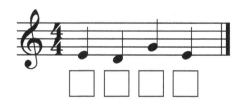

The Bass Clef

The BASS CLEF SIGN 𝄢 locates the F below the middle of the keyboard.

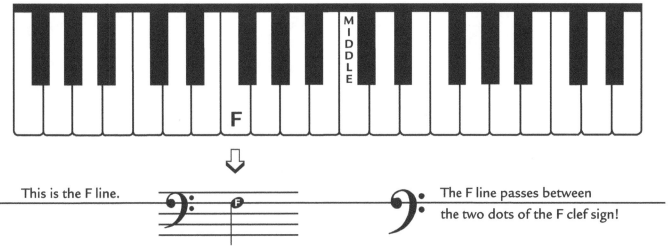

This is the F line.

The F line passes between the two dots of the F clef sign!

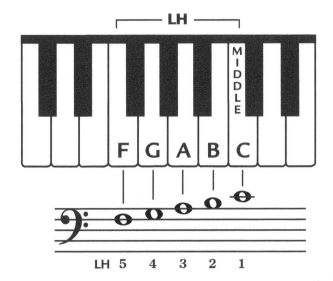

By moving up or down from the F line, you can name any note on the bass staff.

1. Write the name of each note in the square below it. Then play and say the note names.

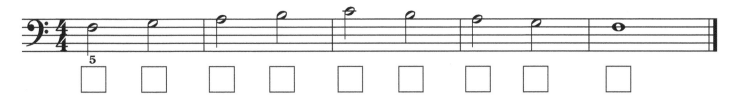

2. Write the name of each note in the square below it. The letters in each group of squares will spell a familiar word.

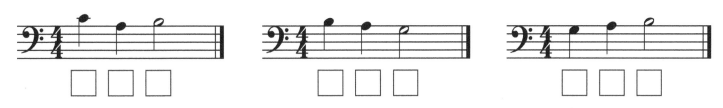

Use with Book 1, page 34.

Skips

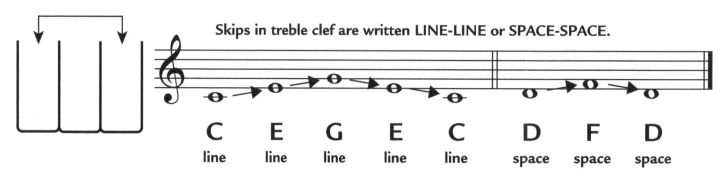

Skips in treble clef are written LINE-LINE or SPACE-SPACE.

C	E	G	E	C	D	F	D
line	line	line	line	line	space	space	space

1. Circle each skip in treble clef.

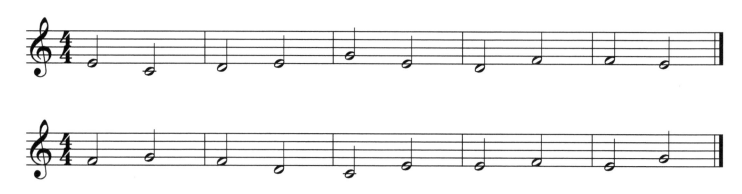

Skips in bass clef are also written LINE-LINE or SPACE-SPACE.

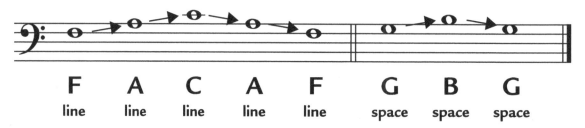

F	A	C	A	F	G	B	G
line	line	line	line	line	space	space	space

2. Circle each skip in bass clef.

The Grand Staff

The TREBLE STAFF and the BASS STAFF are joined together
with a BRACE and a BAR LINE to make a GRAND STAFF.

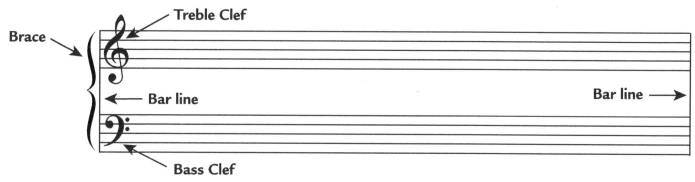

Draw two grand staffs by following these steps:

1. Draw a TREBLE CLEF sign on the top staff.
2. Draw a BASS CLEF sign on the staff just below it.
3. Draw a BAR LINE at the beginning and end of the two staffs.
4. Draw a BRACE at the beginning of the two staffs.

Use with Book 1, page 37.

The Half Rest

A *half rest* means to be silent for two counts.

How to Draw Half Rests

Step 1: Trace the box on top of the middle line of the staff.

Step 2: Fill in the box.

Draw five more half rests.

Note and Rest Review

Draw a line connecting the dots to match the note
with the rest that gets the same number of counts.

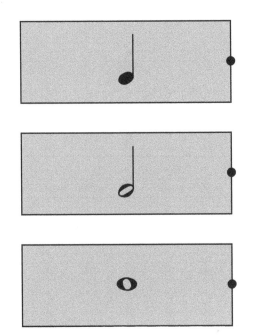

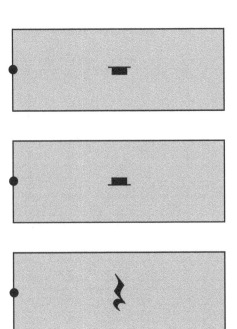

Middle C Position for LH

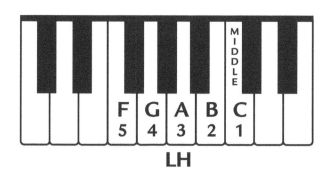

LH

1. Write the names of the keys in the LH MIDDLE C POSITION on the keyboard.

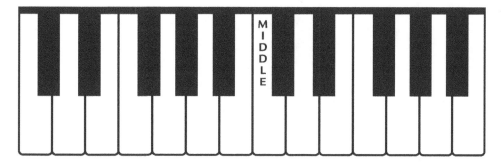

2. Draw lines connecting the dots to match the LH finger number with the key that it plays in MIDDLE C POSITION.

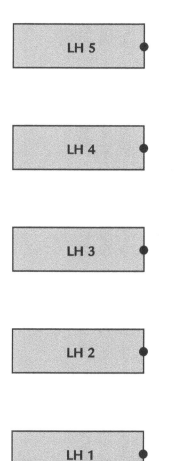

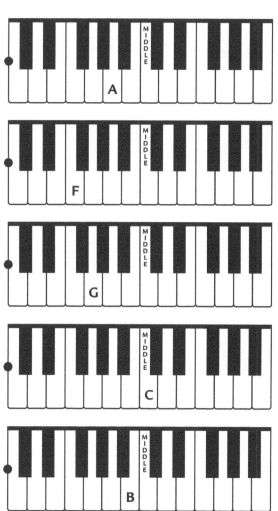

Use with Book 1, page 40.

Middle C Position for RH

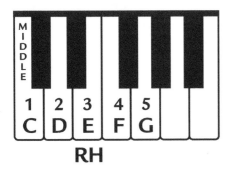

RH

1. Write the names of the keys in the RH MIDDLE C POSITION on the keyboard.

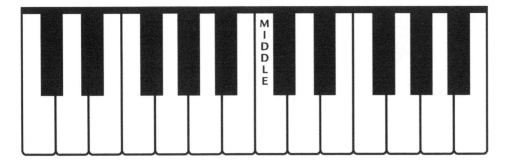

2. Draw lines connecting the dots to match the RH finger number with the key that it plays in MIDDLE C POSITION.

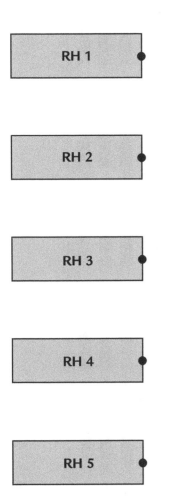

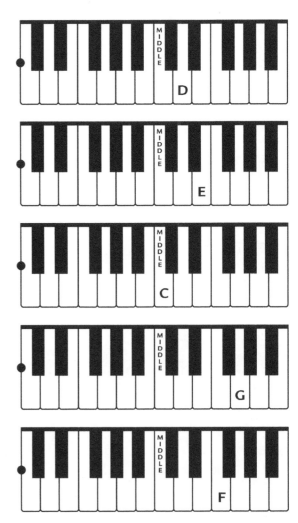

Use with Book 1, page 42.

C Position for LH

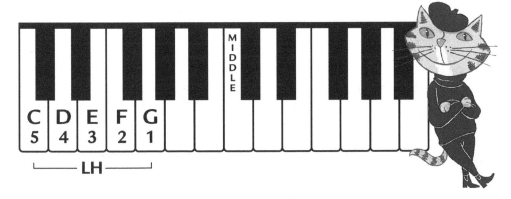

1. Write the names of the keys in the LH C POSITION on the keyboard.

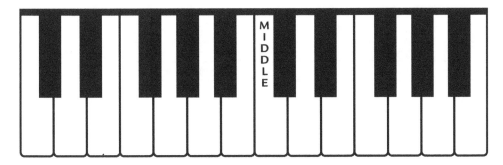

2. Draw lines connecting the dots to match the LH finger number with the key that it plays in C POSITION.

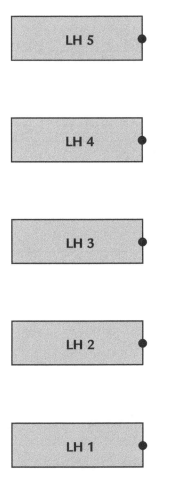

LH 5

LH 4

LH 3

LH 2

LH 1

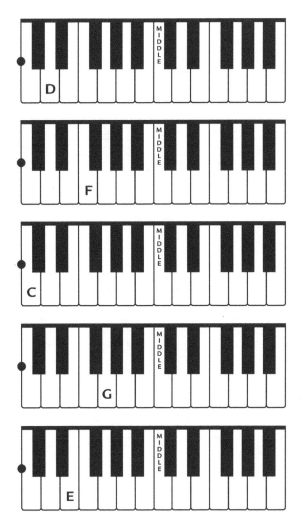

Use with Book 1, page 43.

C Position on the Grand Staff

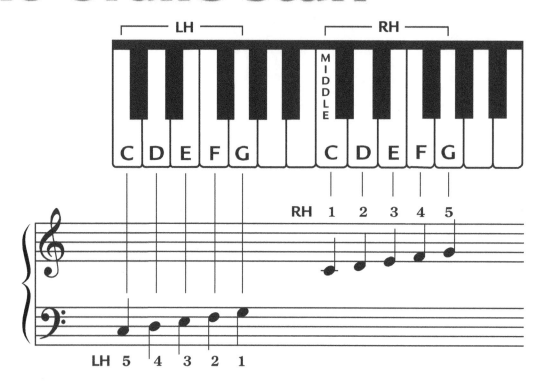

1. Circle each of the LH and RH notes from the C position on the Grand Staff.

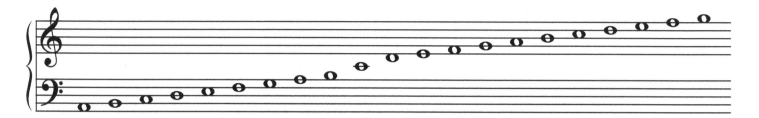

2. Write the name of each note in the square below it. Then play and say the note names.

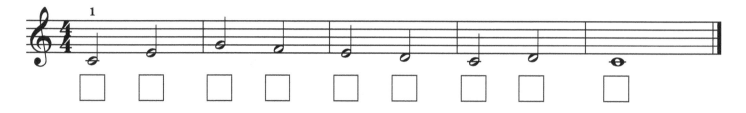

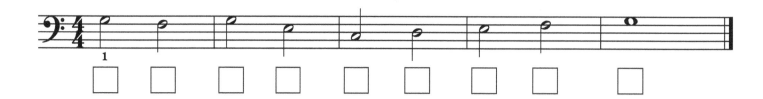

More C Position on the Grand Staff

1. Print the letter names for both the LH and RH C POSITION on the keyboard.
2. Draw a line to connect each note on the staff to the appropriate key on the keyboard.

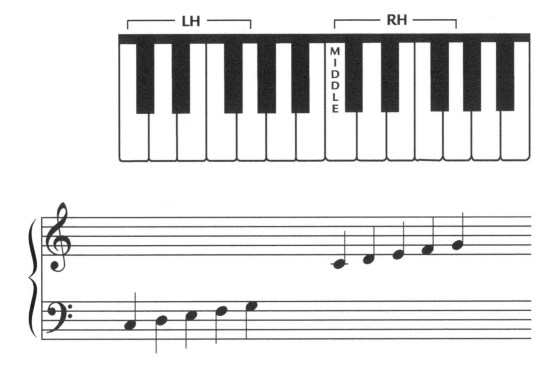

3. Draw lines connecting the dots on the matching boxes.

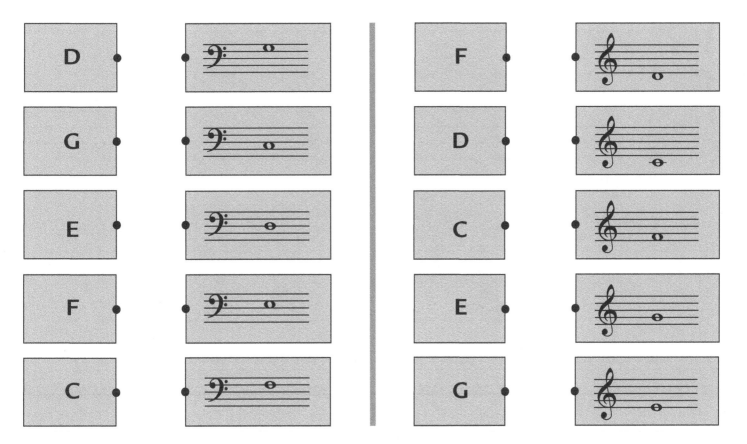

Use with Book 2, page 5.

Middle C Position on the Grand Staff

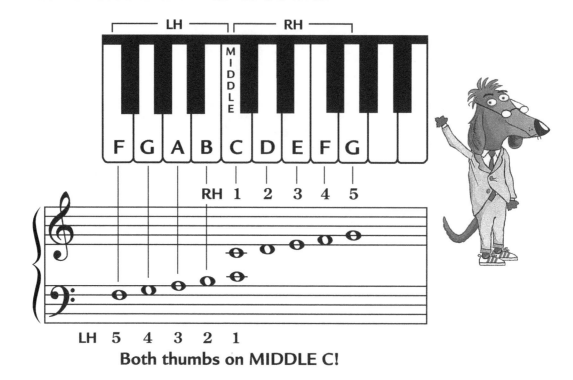

Both thumbs on MIDDLE C!

1. Using whole notes, draw the LH notes from the Middle C Position in the BASS staff under the squares.

2. Using whole notes, draw the RH notes from the Middle C Position in the TREBLE staff over the squares.

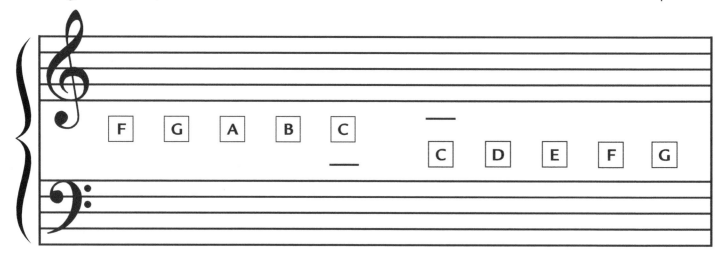

3. Write the name of each note in the square below it. Then play and say the note names.

More Middle C Position on the Grand Staff

1. Print the letter names for both the LH and RH MIDDLE C POSITION on the keyboard below.

2. Draw a line to connect each note on the staff to the appropriate key on the keyboard.

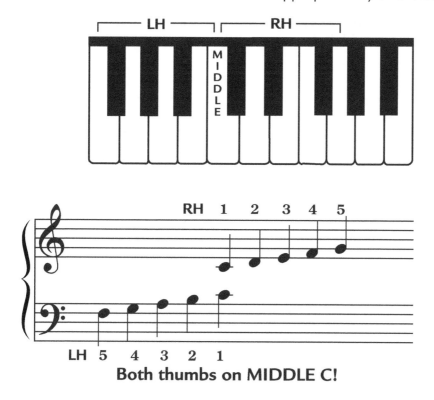

Both thumbs on MIDDLE C!

3. Draw lines connecting the dots on the matching boxes.

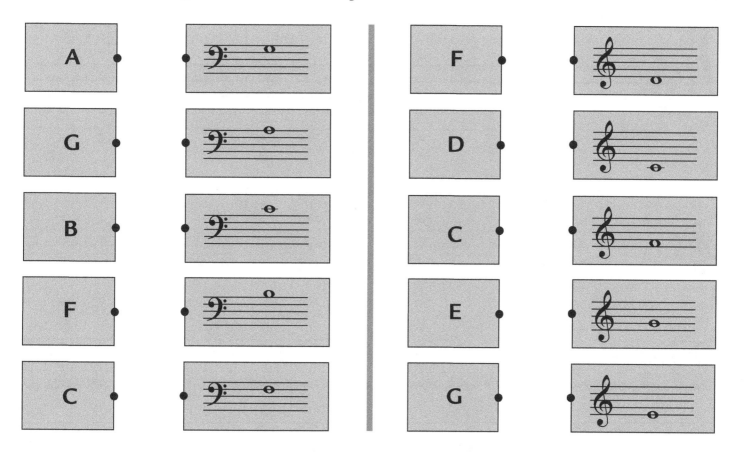

Use with Book 2, page 9.

C Position Review

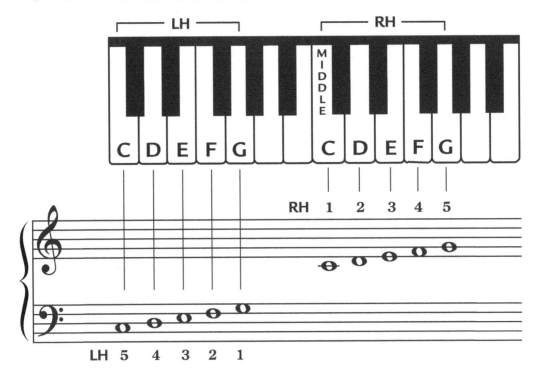

1. Using whole notes, draw the LH notes from C Position in the BASS staff under the squares.

2. Using whole notes, draw the RH notes from C Position in the TREBLE staff over the squares.

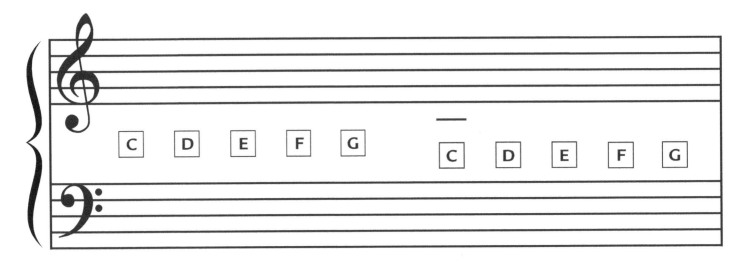

3. Write the name of each note in the square below it. Then play and say the note names.

Review

Draw a line connecting the dots to match the symbol to its name.

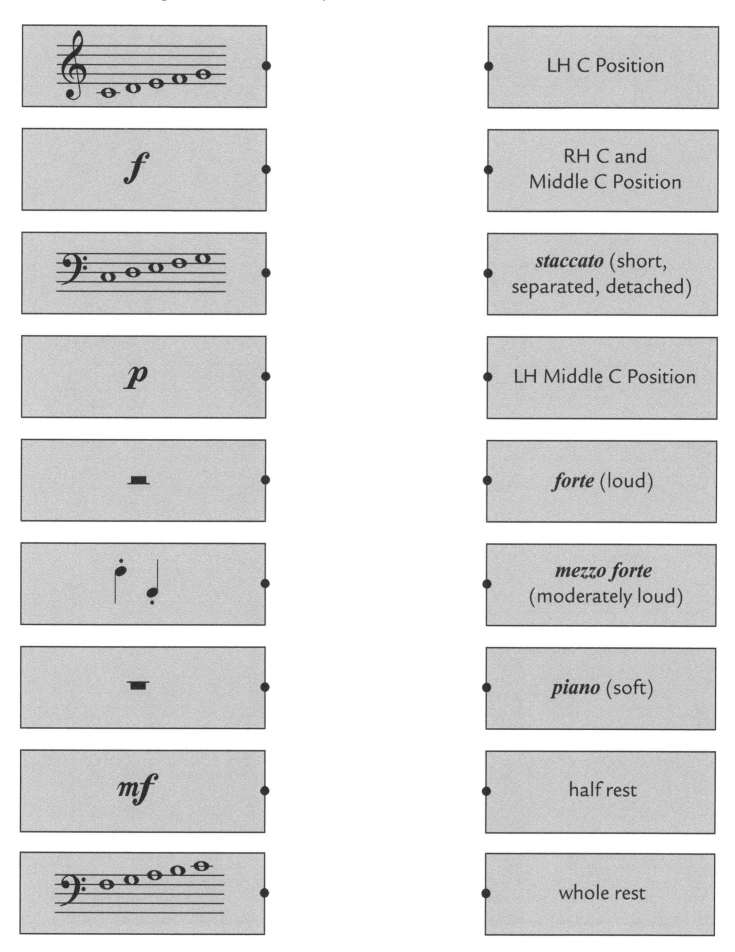

Use with Book 2, page 12.

2nds

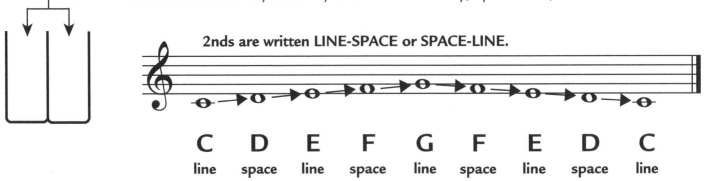

The distance from any white key to the next white key, up or down, is called a **2nd.**

2nds are written LINE-SPACE or SPACE-LINE.

C	D	E	F	G	F	E	D	C
line	space	line	space	line	space	line	space	line

1. Draw a whole note UP a 2nd from the given note in each example below.
2. Write the name of each note in the square below it.

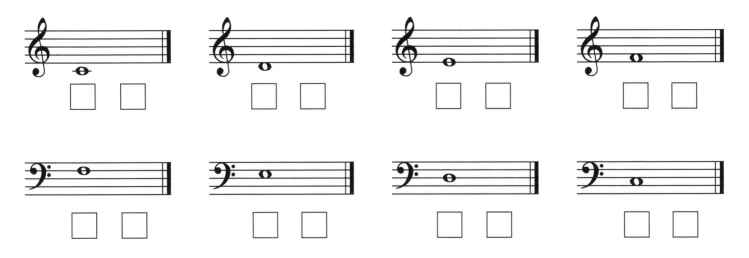

3. Draw a whole note DOWN a 2nd from the given note in each example below.
4. Write the name of each note in the square below it.

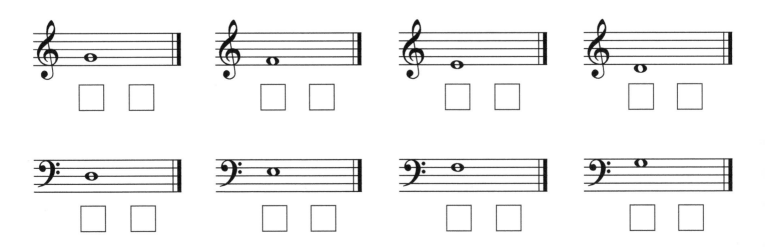

Use with Book 2, page 13.

3rds

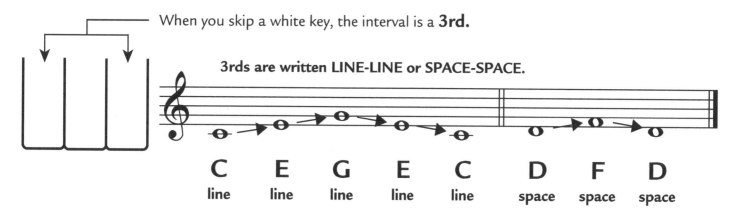

When you skip a white key, the interval is a **3rd.**

3rds are written LINE-LINE or SPACE-SPACE.

C E G E C D F D
line line line line line space space space

1. Draw a whole note UP a 3rd from the given note in each example below.
2. Write the name of each note in the square below it.

3. Draw a whole note DOWN a 3rd from the given note in each example below.
4. Write the name of each note in the square below it.

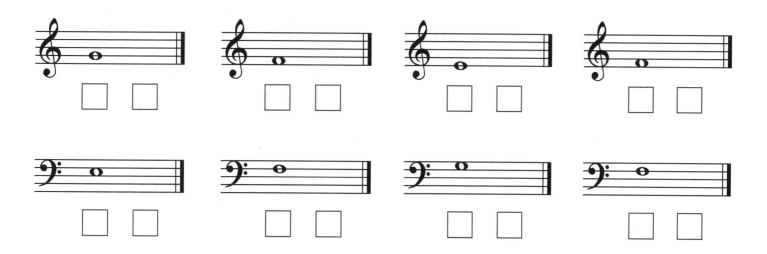

Use with Book 2, page 16.

Melodic Intervals

Notes played SEPARATELY make a MELODY.

Intervals between these notes are MELODIC INTERVALS.

1. Write the names of the MELODIC INTERVALS (2nd or 3rd) in the boxes.

2. In the exercises below, identify the MELODIC INTERVALS in the C Position.
   - If the interval moves UP, write UP in the higher box above the staff.
   - If it moves DOWN, write DOWN in the higher box.
   - Write the name of the interval (2nd or 3rd) in the lower box.

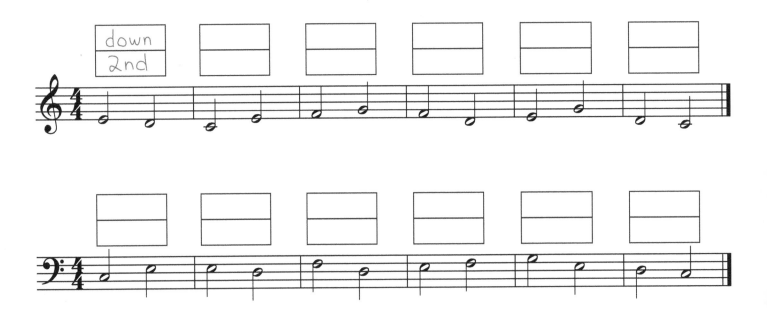

Harmonic Intervals

Notes played TOGETHER make HARMONY.

Intervals between these notes are HARMONIC INTERVALS.

1. Write the names of the HARMONIC INTERVALS (2nd or 3rd) in the boxes.

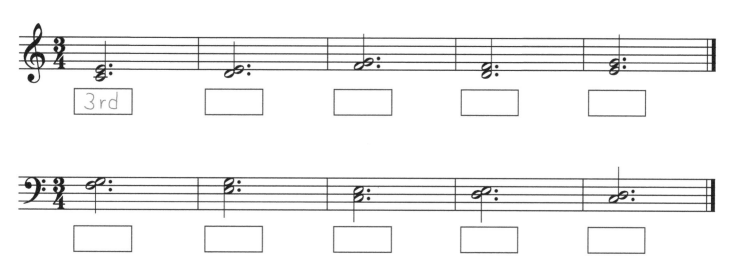

3rd

2. In the exercises below, write the names of the notes in the squares above the staff.
   Write the name of the lower note in the lower square; the name of the higher note
   in the higher square.

3. Write the names of the HARMONIC INTERVALS (2nd or 3rd) in the boxes below
   the staff.

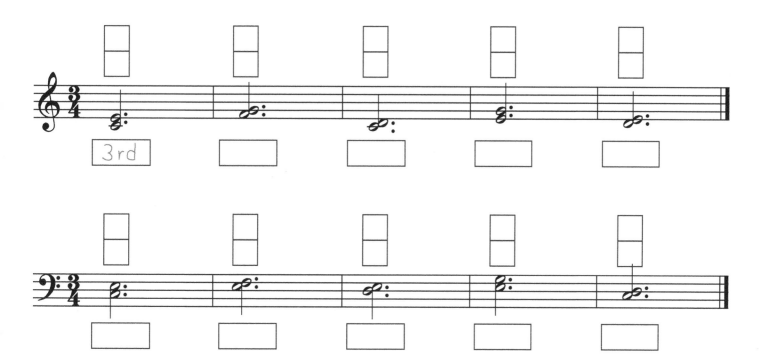

3rd

Use with Book 2, page 19.

4ths

When you skip two white keys, the interval is a **4th**.

4ths are written LINE-SPACE or SPACE-LINE.

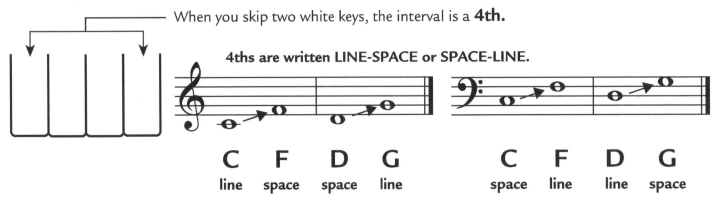

| C | F | D | G | C | F | D | G |
| line | space | space | line | space | line | line | space |

1. Draw a whole note UP a 4th from the given note in each example below.
2. Write the name of each note in the square below it.

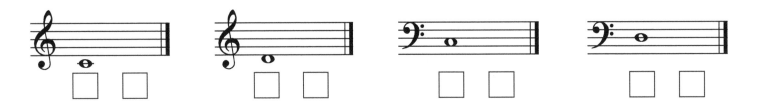

3. Draw a whole note DOWN a 4th from the given note in each example below.
4. Write the name of each note in the square below it.

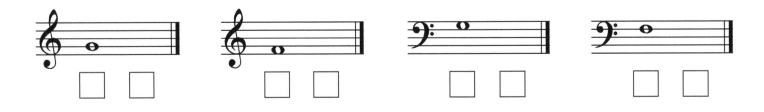

5. Circle each HARMONIC 4th.

Note and Interval Review

1. Write the name of each note in the square below it.

2. Using whole notes, draw the notes from the MIDDLE C POSITION in the TREBLE STAFF under the squares.

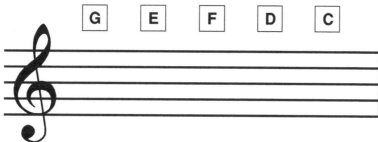

3. Using whole notes, draw the notes from the MIDDLE C POSITION in the BASS STAFF under the squares.

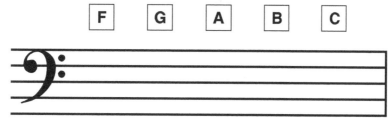

4. Draw a half note UP from the given note in each measure below to make the indicated melodic interval. Turn all the stems in the treble clef UP. Turn all the stems in the bass clef DOWN.

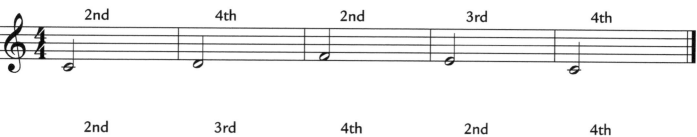

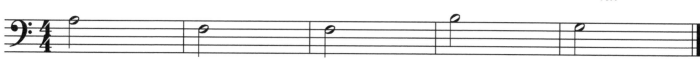

Use with Book 2, page 25.

5ths

When you skip three white keys, the interval is a **5th.**

5ths are written LINE-LINE or SPACE-SPACE.

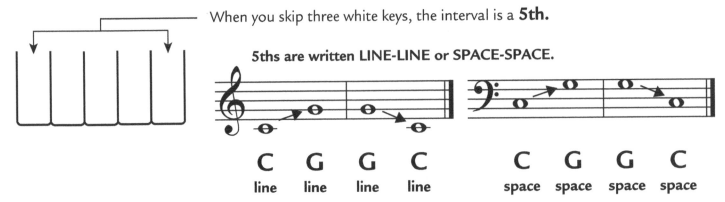

C	G	G	C	C	G	G	C
line	line	line	line	space	space	space	space

1. Draw a half note UP a 5th from each C and DOWN a 5th from each G on each staff below.

2. Write the name of each note in the square below it.

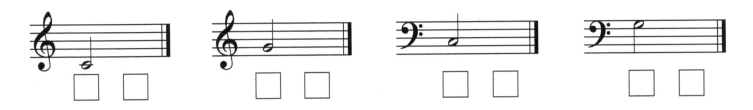

3. Draw a whole note ABOVE the given note in each measure below to make the indicated harmonic interval.

4. Write the names of the notes in the squares. Write the name of the lower note in the lower square; the name of the higher note in the higher square.

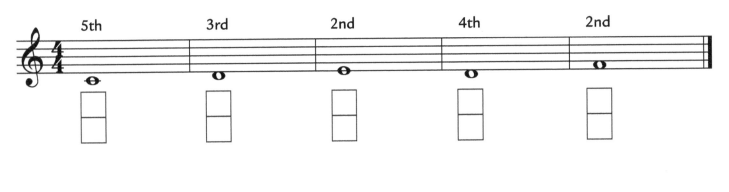

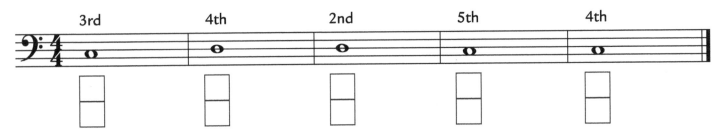

Note and Interval Review

1. Write the name of each note in the square below it.

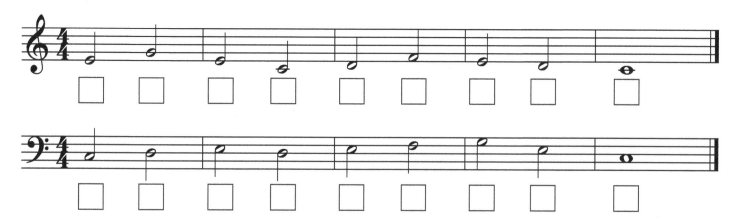

2. Using whole notes, draw the notes from the C POSITION in the TREBLE STAFF under the squares.

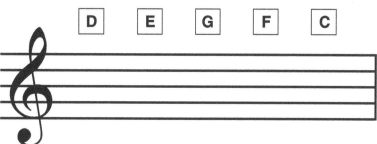

3. Using whole notes, draw the notes from the C POSITION in the BASS STAFF under the squares.

4. Draw a half note UP from the given note in each measure below to make the indicated melodic interval. Turn all the stems in the treble clef UP. Turn all the stems in the bass clef DOWN.

Use with Book 2, page 30.

G-A-B in Treble Clef

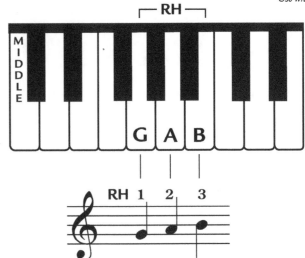

1. Using quarter notes, draw G five more times.

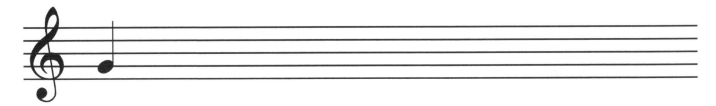

2. Using half notes, draw A five more times.

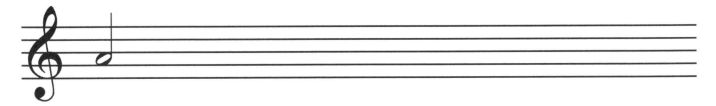

3. Using whole notes, draw B five more times.

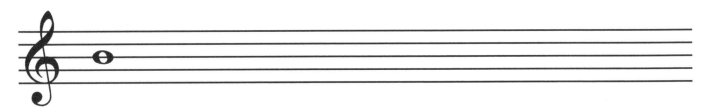

4. Draw lines connecting the dots on the matching boxes.

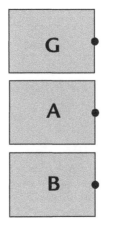

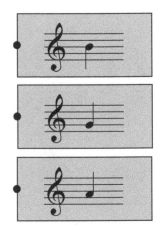

G-A-B in Bass Clef

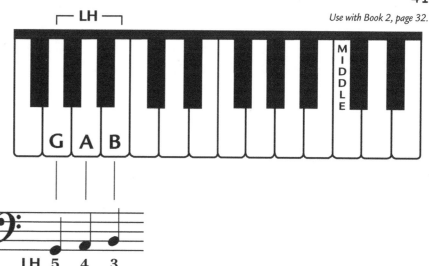

1. Using whole notes, draw G five more times.

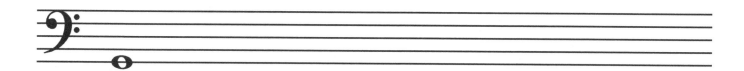

2. Using half notes, draw A five more times.

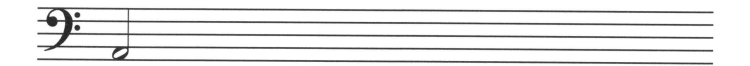

3. Using quarter notes, draw B five more times.

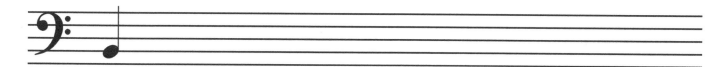

4. Draw lines connecting the dots on the matching boxes.

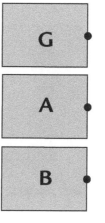

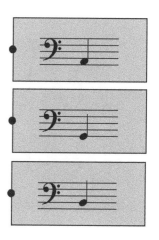

Use with Book 2, page 34.

G Position for RH

1. Print the letter names for the RH G POSITION on the keyboard.

2. Draw a line to connect each note on the staff to the appropriate key on the keyboard.

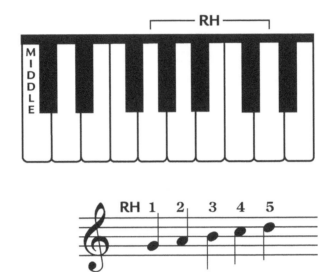

3. Draw lines connecting the dots on the matching boxes.

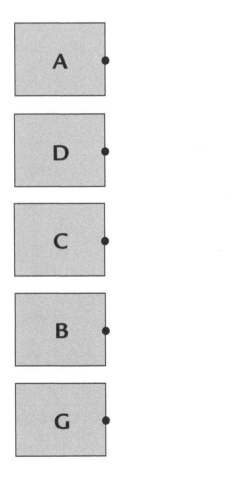

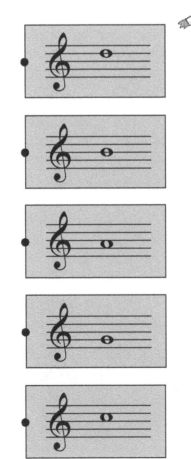

G Position for LH

1. Print the letter names for the LH G POSITION on the keyboard.

2. Draw a line to connect each note on the staff to the appropriate key on the keyboard.

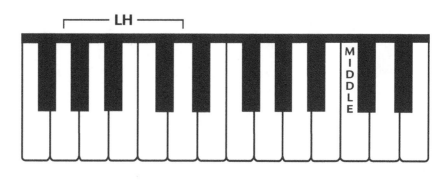

3. Draw lines connecting the dots on the matching boxes.

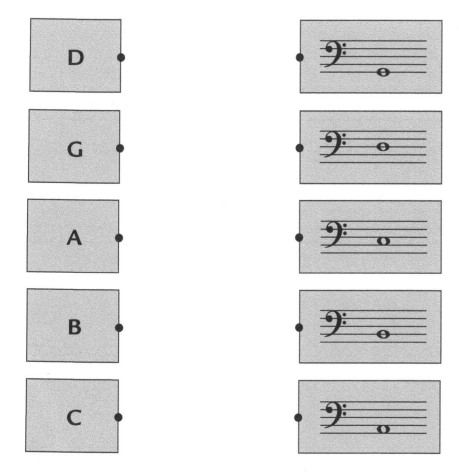

Use with Book 2, page 36.

G Position on the Grand Staff

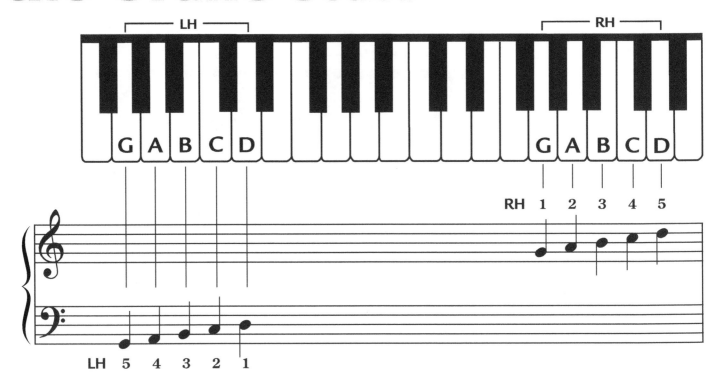

1. Using whole notes, draw the LH notes from G Position in the BASS staff under the squares.

2. Using whole notes, draw the RH notes from G Position in the TREBLE staff over the squares.

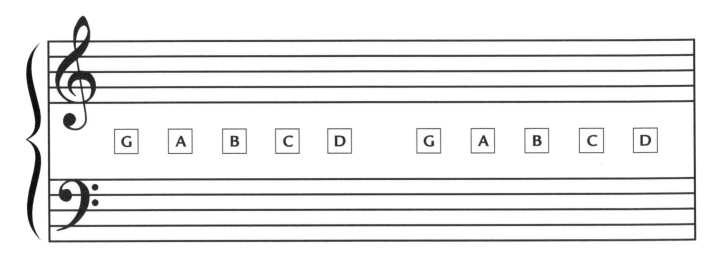

3. Write the name of each note in the square below it. Then play and say the note names.

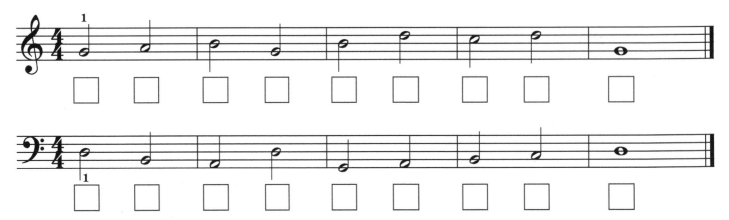

1. Draw a FLAT (♭) before each B on the staffs below.

2. Write the name of each note in the square below it.

3. Draw lines connecting the dots, to match the name of the flatted note to its location on the keytboard.

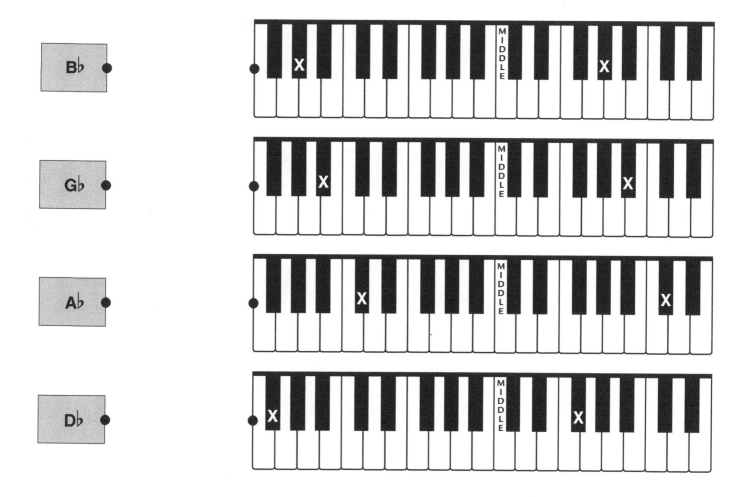

Use with Book 2, page 42.

Sharp

1. Draw a SHARP (♯) before each C on the staffs below.

2. Write the name of each note in the square below it.

3. Draw lines connecting the dots, to match the name of the flatted note to its location on the keytboard.

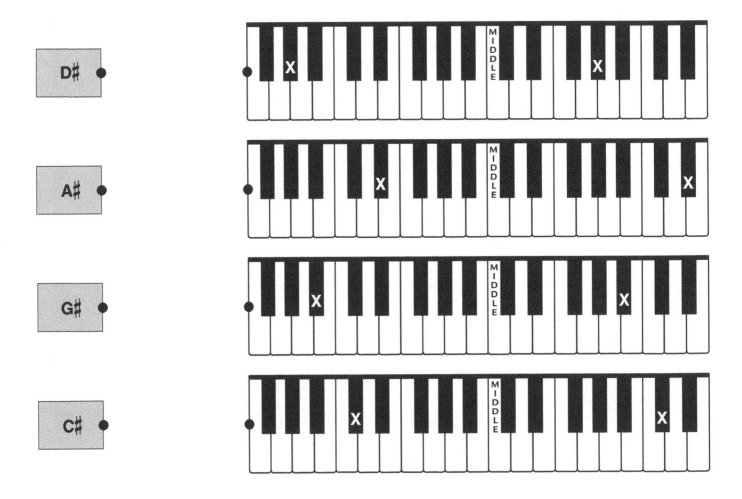

Note and Interval Review in Treble Clef

1. Draw lines connecting the dots to the matching boxes.

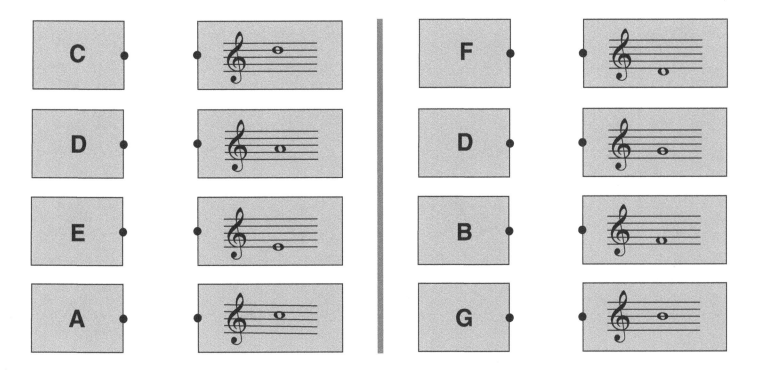

2. Draw a half note BELOW the given note to make the indicated melodic interval. Turn all the stems UP.

3. Write the name of each note in the square below it.

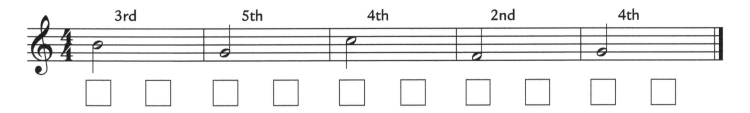

4. Draw a whole note ABOVE the given note to make the indicated harmonic interval.

5. Write the names of the notes in the squares. Write the name of the lower note in the lower square; the name of the higher note in the higher square.

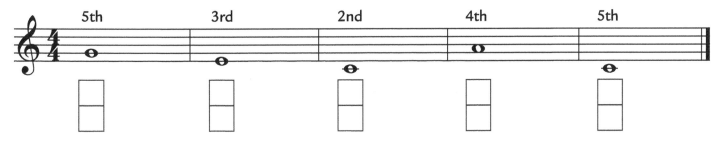

Use with Book 2, page 46.

Note and Interval Review in Bass Clef

1. Draw lines connecting the dots to the matching boxes.

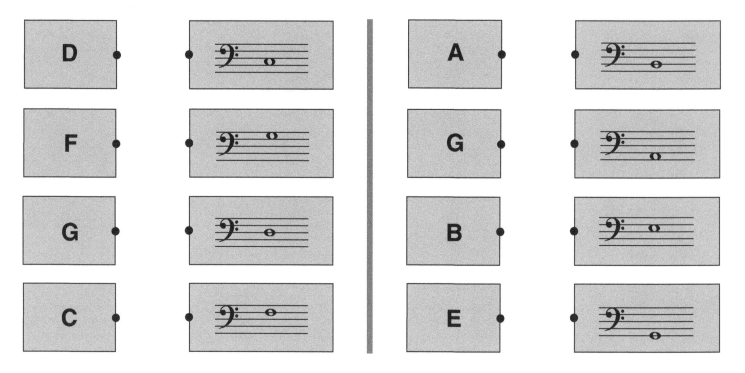

2. Draw a half note BELOW the given note to make the indicated melodic interval. Turn all the stems UP.

3. Write the name of each note in the square below it.

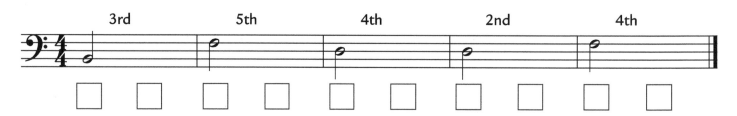

4. Draw a whole note ABOVE the given note to make the indicated harmonic interval.

5. Write the names of the notes in the squares. Write the name of the lower note in the lower square; the name of the higher note in the higher square.

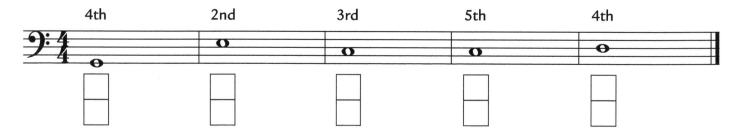